Dear Parent:

Congratulations! Your child is taking the first steps on an exciting journey. The destination? Independent reading!

STEP INTO READING® will help your child get there. The program offers five steps to reading success. Each step includes fun stories and colorful art. There are also Step into Reading Sticker Books, Step into Reading Math Readers, Step into Reading Write-In Readers, Step into Reading Phonics Readers, and Step into Reading Phonics First Steps! Boxed Sets—a complete literacy program with something for every child.

Learning to Read, Step by Step!

Ready to Read Preschool–Kindergarten
• big type and easy words • rhyme and rhythm • picture clues
For children who know the alphabet and are eager to begin reading.

Reading with Help   Preschool–Grade 1
• basic vocabulary • short sentences • simple stories
For children who recognize familiar words and sound out new words with help.

Reading on Your Own Grades 1–3
• engaging characters • easy-to-follow plots • popular topics
For children who are ready to read on their own.

Reading Paragraphs Grades 2–3
• challenging vocabulary • short paragraphs • exciting stories
For newly independent readers who read simple sentences with confidence.

Ready for Chapters Grades 2–4
• chapters • longer paragraphs • full-color art
For children who want to take the plunge into chapter books but still like colorful pictures.

STEP INTO READING® is designed to give every child a successful reading experience. The grade levels are only guides. Children can progress through the steps at their own speed, developing confidence in their reading, no matter what their grade.

Remember, a lifetime love of reading starts with a single step!

For Katie Claire Gisondi & Jack Gisondi,
two unforgettable little treats
—F.M.

To Mary, with love
—R.W.

Author acknowledgments: Thanks to Bryan Craig, research librarian at Monticello, for his expertise. Thanks to my talented editor and collaborator, Shana Corey, for her patience and creativity. Thanks to Angela Roberts for her assistance. And thanks to Mark Klein for finding that apple picker!

Photo credits: Portrait of Thomas Jefferson © Burstein Collection/CORBIS. Macaroni-making machine courtesy of the Library of Congress.

www.stepintoreading.com

Educators and librarians, for a variety of teaching tools, visit us at
www.randomhouse.com/teachers

Library of Congress Cataloging-in-Publication Data
Murphy, Frank.
Thomas Jefferson's feast / by Frank Murphy ; illustrated by Richard Walz.
    p.   cm. — (Step into reading. A step 4 book)
SUMMARY: Tells of Thomas Jefferson's trip to France in 1784, and all the exotic foods he learned about and then introduced to America, including ice cream, macaroni and cheese, and tomatoes.
ISBN 0-375-82289-5 (trade) — ISBN 0-375-92289-X (lib. bdg.)
1. Jefferson, Thomas, 1743–1826—Juvenile literature.   2. Jefferson, Thomas, 1743–1826—
Journeys—France—Juvenile literature.   3. Presidents—United States—Biography—Juvenile
literature.   4. Food—History—18th century—Juvenile literature.   5. Cookery, French—
History—18th century—Juvenile literature.   [1. Jefferson, Thomas, 1743–1826.   2. Presidents.
3. Food—History.]   I. Walz, Richard, ill.   II. Title.   III. Series: Step into reading. Step 4 book.
E332.79 .M87 2003 394.1'0973—dc21 2002014219

Printed in the United States of America   First Edition
10 9 8 7 6 5 4 3

Thomas Jefferson's
FEAST

by Frank Murphy
illustrated by Richard Walz

Random House 🏠 New York

Long ago, before your great-great-grandparents were born, there lived a man named Thomas Jefferson. You probably know his name because he was the third president of the United States.

But that's not all there is to know about Thomas Jefferson.

Thomas Jefferson loved to read.

He collected books about the stars and books about history. In fact, he had one of the largest libraries in America.

Thomas Jefferson also loved to write.

He wrote letters to people like Benjamin Franklin and George Washington. In his lifetime, he wrote over *20,000* letters. That's like writing a letter a day, every day, for 55 years!

Many of Thomas's letters said that America should be its own country. (The British thought America belonged to them.)

So Thomas Jefferson went to work writing the Declaration of Independence. He wrote and rewrote it for 17 days straight—until he got it just right.

When in the people

Of course, with all that reading and writing and thinking, sometimes Thomas Jefferson got tired.

Sometimes his back hurt.

And sometimes he got hungry. When that happened . . .

. . . he usually took a break and had a snack. Because Thomas Jefferson really, *really* loved food!

Thomas liked food *so* much, he
sometimes spent as much as 50 dollars
on groceries in just one day! (That would
be like spending *750* dollars today!)

Thomas also spent a lot of time *thinking* about food. He even thought about better ways to get food!

Sometimes Thomas Jefferson got hungry late at night after everyone else had gone to bed.

When that happened, he had to tiptoe down the hallway and all the way downstairs to the kitchen.

Then he had to fix a tray of food and carry it *all* the way back upstairs and down the long, dark hallway to the dining room.

If he was lucky, there was still a little left when he sat down to eat.

Thomas needed an easier way to get his food upstairs.

So he built a little elevator in his house. It was too small to carry people. But it could take food and drinks from the kitchen to the dining room upstairs—without spilling a drop! Thomas called his invention a dumbwaiter.

Thomas's dumbwaiter is still in his house in Virginia today—and it *still* works!

Thomas had a giant garden behind his house. The garden was 1,000 feet long. It was filled with more than 200 different kinds of fruits and vegetables.

If you visit Thomas's house, Monticello,
today, you can still see many of the fruit
trees he planted.

Sometimes Thomas wanted a snack from his garden. But the apples on the bottoms of the trees were usually already picked.

"Hmmm," thought Thomas. "There must be a simple way to get apples from the tops of the trees."

Thomas found a long wooden pole. He attached a metal basket to it. The basket had hooks at the top.

He used the hooks to pull off the apples. Presto! Ripe apples fell into the basket!

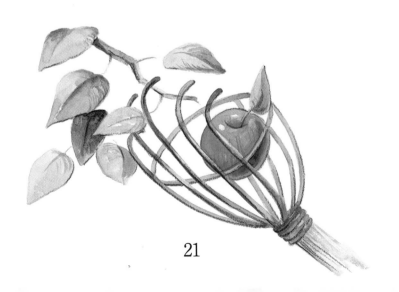

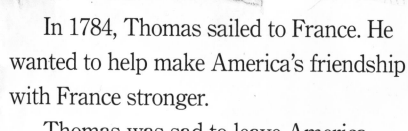

In 1784, Thomas sailed to France. He wanted to help make America's friendship with France stronger.

Thomas was sad to leave America and Monticello. But he knew it was an important job. He also knew there would be *lots* of new foods to try!

Thomas was right!

In between meetings, he tasted macaroni covered with cheese!

He munched on potatoes fried in the French manner.

One night, he went to a dinner party.
"Hello!" said Thomas.

"Bonjour!" said his host. (*Bonjour* means "hello" in French.)

Thomas's host offered him a special dessert. It was ice cream wrapped in a warm pie crust. Ice cream hadn't come to America yet.

For *bonjour,* say: bohn-JOOR

Thomas took a bite.

"Good!" said Thomas.

"Bon!" said his host. (*Bon* means "good" in French.)

For *bon,* say: bohn

During his visit, Thomas saw a
Frenchman eating a bright red fruit.
It was called a *pomme d'amour*. (That
means "love apple" in French.) Thomas
had seen the fruit before. But in America
it was usually just used for decoration.
Most people thought it was poison, so no
one ate it.

The Frenchman promised it was not
poison. So Thomas took a bite.

Thomas *loved* the love apple!

28

For *pomme d'amour*, say: pohm dah-MOOR

29

Thomas stayed in France for five years. When it was time for him to go back to America, he couldn't wait to share all his new favorite foods!

He wrote down the recipes for macaroni and cheese, fried potatoes, and ice cream. He even decided to plant some love apples at Monticello.

He waved goodbye to his French friends and got on the ship.

"*Au revoir!*" he said. (*Au revoir* means "goodbye" in French.)

For *au revoir*, say: oh ruh-VWAHR

"How was France?" everyone asked when Thomas got home.

"Delicious!" answered Thomas.

He decided to have a feast to show off the new foods.

Of course, that was easier said than done.

Thomas planted love apple seeds—

and waited for them to grow.

He drew a picture of a macaroni-making machine he had seen in France. Then he sent a friend all the way to Italy to buy one. (Thomas had heard that Italy had the best macaroni-making machines!)

He dug up potatoes from his garden.

Finally, he made ice cream. This was *not* easy. First he mixed cream and eggs and sugar. He packed it with ice and salt.

Then he stirred and stirred *and stirred*.

At last, everything was ready. The love apples were ripe. The macaroni was cheesy. The potatoes were crisp. The ice cream was icy.

"Perfect!" said Thomas.

Thomas invited all his friends.

"What's for dinner?" they asked.

"It's a surprise," said Thomas. "Let's eat!"

Thomas's guests loved the feast! They gobbled up the macaroni and cheese. They ate every last fried potato. They asked for more of Thomas's ice cream. They even asked for the recipes.

When they were about to go home,
Thomas noticed something. No one had
touched their love apples! Everyone
believed they were poison.

"Try them," Thomas begged.

"No thanks," everyone said. "We're full."

Thomas felt terrible! How could he get
people to try love apples?

The next day Thomas rode into the town of Lynchburg to visit a friend. He noticed a few love apples growing in her yard. Suddenly, Thomas had an idea!

He asked if he could pick a few love apples. His friend said yes.

Thomas walked down the street with the love apples.

He raised one to his mouth. People stopped and pointed. "What are you doing?" they shouted. "That's poison! Stop!"

Thomas took a bite.

"Oh no!" everyone said. "Save him! He's going to get sick!"

But Thomas didn't get sick.

He just kept eating.

Pretty soon, people got curious about the love apples. They tried them themselves. *"Scrumptious!"* everyone said.

And to this day, Americans enjoy eating love apples. (Especially on pizza!)

Today, we still eat many of the foods Thomas Jefferson brought from France. Only now we call "potatoes fried in the French manner" French fries. And we call love apples tomatoes!

(Macaroni and cheese is still called macaroni and cheese, and ice cream is still called ice cream!)

AUTHOR'S NOTE

Thomas Jefferson stayed in France from 1784 to 1789. He may not have served all the foods in this book at one party. But he really did introduce them to America. And he was well known for his fancy dinner parties. So it just may have happened this way.

Thomas Jefferson also really did have a pet mockingbird that flew around his study. His name was Dick.

Thomas Jefferson

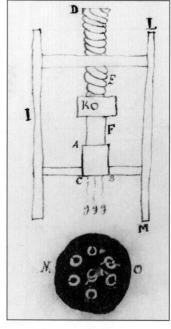

Thomas Jefferson's drawing of a macaroni-making machine